AF143886

BOOK ANALYSIS

Written by Scéona Poroli-Duwez
Translated by Rebecca Neal

The Girl Who Played Go
BY SHAN SA

SHAN SA

- **Born in Beijing in 1972.**
- **Notable works:**
  - *The Four Lives of the Willow* (1999), novel
  - *The Girl Who Played Go* (2001), novel
  - *Empress* (2003), novel

Shan Sa (a pseudonym meaning "whistle of the wind in the mountains") was born in Beijing in 1972. In 1990, after the Tiananmen Square protests, she decided to leave China for Paris in order to begin a new life in France. Thanks to a scholarship from the French government, she was able to take the baccalaureate examination and go on to study philosophy.

She found success as a poet and writer from a very early age: in 1984, aged just 12, she won first prize in the Chinese national poetry contest for children, and her first novel *Porte de la paix celeste* ("Gate of the Heavenly Peace", 1997) won

France's prestigious Prix Goncourt du Premier Roman, which aims to recognise the best debut novel of the year.

The Girl Who Played Go (2001) won the Prix Goncourt des Lycéens, which is voted on by secondary school students from across France, cementing Shan Sa's place as a key figure on the French literary scene.

THE GIRL WHO PLAYED GO

CULTURE SHOCK AND ITS TRAGIC CONSEQUENCES

- **Genre:** novel
- **Reference edition:** Shan Sa (2004) *The Girl Who Played Go*. Trans. Hunter, A. New York: Vintage.
- **1st edition:** 2001
- **Themes:** war, death, love, coming of age, China, games, rebellion

The Girl Who Played Go was published in 2001 and met with resounding success: it sold over 100 000 copies, won the Prix Goncourt des Lycéens and garnered widespread critical acclaim.

The novel tells the story of two characters who form a connection against all odds. One of them is a proud, independent 16-year-old Chinese girl, while the other is a Japanese solider who is determined to defend his country and his honour.

They meet against the backdrop of the Second Sino-Japanese War (1937-1945), and as they play go together, the reader witnesses the inevitable culture clash and the blossoming of a doomed love.

SUMMARY

The story is set in Manchuria, north-east China, at the heart of the Second Sino-Japanese War, which broke out in 1937. Song of the Night is a young Chinese girl and an excellent go player: she is "the only woman to be admitted into the exclusive society of true enthusiasts" (p. 28) and has just won her hundredth victory in the Square of a Thousand Winds. Irritated by her cousin Lu's desire to marry her, she decides to wager their marriage on a game of go. Lu loses and heads back to Peking.

GOOD TO KNOW

In 1937, six years after its invasion of Manchuria, the Imperial Japanese Army conquered eastern China as part of its policy of territorial expansion. The Second Sino-Japanese War (1937-1945) was particularly deadly, and its early stages saw the Empire of Japan crush the Chinese troops, notably at Nanking, the capital of the Republic of China.

However, foreign powers were quick to intervene in the conflict, and in 1945 Japan, backed by the USSR, was defeated by China, which had the support of the USA. Losses during the war are estimated at 1.1 million on the Japanese side, compared with 3 million soldiers and 9 million civilians on the Chinese side.

During the New Year celebrations, the go player becomes friends with Huong, one of her classmates. Huong tells Song of the Night about her unhappiness, and in turn the young girl reveals that she cannot accept the fate of the women around her: Huong is about to be forced into an arranged marriage by her father, her sister is in an unhappy relationship with an unfaithful man, and her mother is treated like a slave by her father.

When a rebellion breaks out and the mayor is killed, the go player is swept along by the crowd until two student revolutionaries, Jing and Min, come to her aid. After this episode, the Japanese take back power in the town and Song of the Night realises that she crosses paths with Min every day.

TROUBLE

The young girl finds herself in a love triangle: she kisses Min while they are out walking together, but she and Jing also have feelings for each other whenever they meet. Min and Song of the Night end up becoming lovers. Jing is jealous and cannot hide his anger, which amuses the go player. Min tells her that he wants to marry her, but she laughs in his face.

At the same time, a young Japanese soldier tells his mother that he is leaving for Manchuria, as Japan needs to conquer China. Although he is filled with hatred towards the Chinese terrorists, the soldier refuses to give into to the violent frenzy that is gradually taking hold of his compatriots. His garrison wins a battle after the mass suicide of their Chinese adversaries: "The Japanese had chosen to be glorious in their action, and the Chinese in their deaths" (p. 36).

The soldiers are relieved to arrive in Ha Rebin, a

large city where they will no longer be isolated. The soldier meets a prostitute called Masayo. He remembers a previous relationship with a geisha and reflects on how it ended with the young girl's mizuage ceremony (a ceremony during which the geisha's hair is cut and her virginity is sold to the highest bidder). He was troubled by the girl's distress and could not take her virginity. The Japanese leave Ha Rebin for a small town named A Thousand Winds.

A DIFFICULT DECISION

Song of the Night meets the Japanese soldier in the Square of a Thousand Winds over a game of go. During the match, the soldier watches the young girl and tries to understand her, which proves a challenge ("It is easier for my fellow officers to fly over China than for me to read the thoughts of the girl who plays go", p. 186). The game is left unfinished and postponed until the next day.

In the meantime, the young girl meets Tang, a student who is friends with Min and Jing. When the first signs of tension appear between Min and the go player, Min tells her that Jing is in love with her and asks her to choose between them. However, the young girl refuses: "If I choose one I would have to forego the other, and I would lose them both" (p. 145).

Shortly afterwards, the soldier takes part in an offensive against the Chinese rebels and Min, Jing and Tang are arrested. He is forced to sit in on the brutal interrogation of a young woman, who turns out to be Tang, and cannot stomach it. The revolutionaries are sentenced to death, apart from Jing, who has betrayed his comrades. The go player looks on helplessly as Min, who she knows is in love with Tang, is executed.

She tells her friend Huong that she is pregnant with his child and says that she wants to die. Huong thinks that she should terminate the pregnancy and recommends a potion that can induce a miscarriage. As the soldier's obsession with the young go player intensifies, Captain Nakamura warns him against embarking on a relationship with a Chinese girl, as it can only end in tragedy.

BETRAYAL AND DEATH

The soldier and the young girl meet again to continue their unfinished match. She asks him to go with her to the Hill of the Seven Ruins and to protect her. He agrees and does as he is asked.

The go player meets Jing, who confesses that he betrayed his comrades. He also tells her that Min married Tang in prison and asks her to run away to Peking with him. The young girl tries to take Huong with them. The soldier and Song of the Night see each other for the last time over a game of go. She asks him to help her to leave for Peking, but he refuses.

Jing and the go player run away while the war rages around them. However, when the young girl realises that she is in love with the Japanese soldier, she leaves Jing to return to Manchuria and continue her go match. On the way, she is captured by a group of Japanese soldiers; one of them is her playing partner. He chooses love over duty ("For your sake I'm going to turn my back on this war and betray my own country", p. 279), and kills her before turning his weapon on himself.

CHARACTER STUDY

The go player is a 16-year-old girl. She is a se-condary school student in A Thousand Winds, a small town in Manchuria where she lives with her parents and her older sister Pearl Moon. Her parents are from a rich family from Peking, but they decided to move to England, where the young girl was born, before returning to China.

This melancholy, rebellious young girl feels strongly about the status of women in her era. She refuses to marry her cousin Lu, plays go even though it is a game reserved for men, and is outraged by the fates of her sister, her mother and her friend Huong, all of whom are married to men they do not love. In addition, she has no interest in the frivolities that other girls her age are drawn to.

We are not given a physical description of Song of the Night until later on in the story, when she meets the Japanese soldier: she has a "wide forehead and slanting eyes like two finely drawn willow leaves" (p. 134). Her appearance is androgynous ("Her flat chest and her two plaits suggest all the ambiguity of adolescence, which makes girls look like transvestite boys", p. 135). Her name is only revealed at the end of the novel.

THE JAPANESE SOLDIER

This 24-year-old man is originally from Tokyo. He has been left traumatised by the Great Kantō earthquake of 1923, which devastated the city and killed his father. He is the oldest child in his family, and remains very attached to them. However, he must leave them behind to defend the honour of his country, and he wavers between pride and guilt: "a soldier is a man who destroys his loved ones' happiness" (p. 47). His main worries include death and the desire to preserve the honour of his family and his country.

However, the young man is torn between two cultures, and he gradually becomes aware of this inner conflict. On the one hand, he is filled with patriotism and harbours an abiding hatred towards the Chinese terrorists, but on the other hand he is secretly fascinated by the Chinese people, having learnt their language and customs from his Chinese nanny, who was always able to assuage his fears.

We are not told the Japanese soldier's name, and the go player refers to him simply as "the Stranger". Furthermore, no physical description of him is provided. Not only does he lack a physical image, but he also camouflages himself by donning a disguise so that he can play with the Chinese.

ANALYSIS

A COMING-OF-AGE NOVEL

The Girl Who Played Go is about the coming of age of two characters: Song of the Night and the Japanese soldier. They meet at a key point in their lives, and the reader witnesses how they change.

The genre of the coming-of-age novel, or *Bildungsroman*, emerged in Germany in the late 18th century. Its main theme is the evolution of a naïve, inexperienced character who changes and forges their own identity as the story progresses. Through strong feelings and formative experiences (death, love, betrayal), the protagonist takes an active part in transforming their life.

The go player is a secondary schoolstudent, and when we first meet her she is young, sarcastic, irritable and capricious. She only cares about go, is dismissive of her cousin Lu, who wants to marry her, and refuses to grow up ("He wants me to join the adult world, but he doesn't realize that I think it is a sad place full of vanity, and it frightens me", p. 28).

All that changes when she meets Min and Jing, two student revolutionaries. Through her relationship with them, she discovers romantic relationships and political engagement. She also looks death in the face (she meets Min and Jing the day the mayor is killed, and their relationship comes to an end when Min is executed) and suffers betrayals (Min marries Tang in prison, and Jing betrays his friends). When she has to deal with these events, the young girl grows up and becomes an adult.

When the Japanese soldier is introduced to us, he is a fervent patriot and a soldier by vocation. Even though he is cold and consumed by hatred towards the Chinese, he is an expert in Chinese language and literature, and admits that his Manchurian nanny comforted him when he was struggling with his strict Japanese upbringing.

His coming of age begins when he meets the go player: he even disguises himself, a physical transformation which symbolises the change in his character. He falls in love with the enemy, which makes him "lose [his] normal points of reference" (p. 171): "It has almost made a free man of me, a man who knows nothing of commitment to duty" (*ibid.*). In the end, he gives in to his feelings and stops fighting them.

LOVE AS A GAME

The Girl Who Played Go is also a love story, but it is an unusual kind of love, as it is shaped by a game. The game of go forms the heart of the story, and Song of the Night discovers love through it.

At the start of the novel, she stakes her marriage to her cousin Lu on the game: "If you win, I accept everything you propose. If you lose, we won't see each other again" (p. 19). She wins the match, which has an immediate effect: "The following morning I am told that he has left" (p. 24).

The game also allows its players to put romantic strategies in place. When the young girl finds herself in a love triangle with Min and Jing, she imagines a possible tactic:

> "In this sort of situation in a game of go, the player opts for a third solution: attacking the opponent where he least expects it. When Min comes to get me on the Square of a Thousand

> Winds tomorrow I will pretend not to see him."
> (p. 145)

Her lover Min sees games as pointless, whereas go is at the centre of the young girl's life. Because of this, later on she says: "I never loved him, anyway. [...] But now I see that it was just vanity [...], the vanity of becoming a woman" (p. 267).

Playing go allows her to meet the Japanese soldier, who she falls in love with over a match that seems to go on forever. In spite of the adverse circumstances, the game of go makes love possible, because it is a reflection of the soul: "I know nothing about him except his soul" (pp. 267-268). There is no love without the game and no game without love; the girl reflects that "Having used it on Cousin Lu, Min and Jing, I know my weapon well" (p. 131).

WAR AS A GAME

The Girl Who Played Go is also a war novel which tells the story of the conflict between China and Japan that took place from 1937 to 1945. Like love, the war too is symbolised by the game. Indeed, the semantic fields of the game of go and of war overlap: "our soldiers", "occupying the strategic positions", "conquer the centre", "my opponent", and so on (p. 151).

Furthermore, a Japanese soldier and a young Chinese girl go head to head over a game of go: in spite of themselves, they reenact the war between their countries. They are both aware that they are doing battle, and they understand that go is more than just a game: for example, Captain Nakamura says that "The game of go is just a camouflage: it's there on that square, as they pretend to play their war game, that our enemies are putting together their twisted strategies" (p. 127).

Finally, the two protagonists both fight their own personal battle through the game of go. As the only female go player on the Square of a Thousand Winds, Song of the Night is waging a symbolic war against the status of women in China during her era. Meanwhile, the young Japanese man knows that as a soldier he is worthless, like the pawns he moves during the game:

> "My posting to China has taught me what greatness and what misery a soldier can know:

on orders he moves from one place to the next without knowing where he is going or why. A pawn among many others. He lives and died anonymously in the name of a greater victory. The game of go is changing me into a senior officer who uses his men coldly and with calculation: the stones make their steady progress, many condemned to die for the sake of a wider strategy." (p. 173)

FURTHER REFLECTION

- Based on the content and structure of the novel, would you say that the player and the soldier work together or against one another?
- In what ways is *The Girl Who Played Go* interesting from a historical point of view?
- Study the female characters in the book. What do they tell us about Japanese and Chinese culture at the time the novel is set?
- In your opinion, why is the young girl's name only revealed at the end of the book?
- Study the links between love and betrayal in the book.
- Does Shan Sa incorporate a poetic dimension in *The Girl Who Played Go*?
- Identify the elements that reveal the duality of the character of the Japanese soldier.
- How would you explain the importance accorded to silence in the novel?

We want to hear from you!
Leave a comment on your online library
and share your favourite books on social media!

FURTHER READING

REFERENCE EDITION

- Shan Sa (2004) *The Girl Who Played Go.* Trans. Hunter, A. New York: Vintage.

Bright ≡Summaries.com

More guides to rediscover your love of literature

www.brightsummaries.com

www.brightsummaries.com

Ebook EAN: 9782806296382

Paperback EAN: 9782806296399

Legal Deposit: D/2017/12603/211

Cover: © Primento

Digital conception by Primento, the digital partner of
publishers.